SPEAKING IN PUBLIC

Published in 2012 by New Holland Publishers
London • Sydney • Cape Town • Auckland
First edition published by Seal Books
Revised and updated in 2011 by New Holland Publishers

86 Edgware Road London W2 2EA United Kingdom
1/66 Gibbes Street Chatswood NSW 2067 Australia
Wembley Square, First Floor, Solan Street Gardens, Cape Town 8001 South Africa
218 Lake Road Northcote Auckland New Zealand

A record of this book is held at the National Library of Australia

ISBN 9781742571294

Publisher: Fiona Schultz
Publishing Manager: Lliane Clarke
Designer: Lisa MacKenzie
Production Manager: Olga Dementiev
Printer: Toppan Leefung Printing Ltd

10 9 8 7 6 5 4 3 2 1

SPEAKING IN PUBLIC

Including Committees, Boards and Think Tanks

Frank Alvey and RG Lathey

NEW
HOLLAND

Contents

Part 2: Addressing Committees, Boards and Think Tanks 57

INTRODUCTION

If you are petrified at the thought of having to stand up and 'say a few words,' console yourself with the knowledge that there are thousands like you. And it's for people like you that this book is written.

The first thing you should realise is that most people are *invited* to speak in public. This means that somebody—perhaps the chair of a meeting or a section of the audience—wants you to speak. And if they want you to speak, doesn't it follow that they will be willing to hear what you have to say?

Remember that people are not normally invited to speak just because they are good speakers. They are invited because they will have something of value to say.

It may be that you have had first-hand experience—maybe you know facts and figures that others don't know—perhaps you've stated privately a point of view which the meeting would like to consider.

An invitation to speak is, therefore, a compliment. The audience wants to hear you. Lack of experience should not deter you from making a contribution.

The next thing you should understand is that it doesn't really matter if you are an experienced speaker or a novice. The success of any speech depends on how the audience reacts to it.

How many times have you been bored to tears by a so-called good speaker? Despite their beautiful voice, clear enunciation, and faultless use of the English language it was an effort to stay awake. Perhaps they sounded too pompous—talking down to their audience in a dull and boring fashion. Whatever it was, they didn't get through to you in spite of their ability as a public speaker. People like to hear people. If the speaker doesn't become a real person in their speech the audience will soon lose interest.

SPEAKING AMONG FRIENDS

Usually, when you are first asked to speak it is among your own group—people you know quite well. You know their faults and their good points just as they know yours; this makes it much easier to say a few words. You don't have to be scared of them because you know them.

How many times have you 'held the floor' and expressed your views on politics, football, the cost of living, and the thousand and one questions that adults have to answer? How often have you come home from meetings and complained about the way things were being run, or the fact that nothing seemed to get done?

What's the use of taking it out on your partner or friends after the meeting? Why not get to your feet and say what you've got to say while the meeting is in progress? If you're not afraid to express your ideas and opinions among a few friends, why not repeat them in public?

BE NATURAL AND RELAXED

For the time being, put out of your mind any thought that you are making a speech. When you get to your feet, talk to the meeting just as though you were talking to your friends. If you were able to convince one or two that you had a good idea you may find, to your complete surprise, that you are able to convince the whole meeting not by making a speech, but just by being yourself.

At least you will have had the satisfaction of making your point of view known. And you will have taken the first step towards becoming a public speaker.

LEARNING TO BE A GOOD SPEAKER

You can learn to be a proficient public speaker just as you can learn to do many other things even if you aren't a talkative person. If you are sincere in your desire to learn and set about your task with enthusiasm and with confidence you will be surprised at your own progress.

PURPOSES OF A SPEECH

Every speech should have a definite purpose:

1. to inform or instruct
2. to convince or persuade
3. to arouse people to action
4. to entertain or amuse.

This doesn't mean that a speech which plainly sets out to inform should not also be humorous. It does mean that when the speech is finished, the audience will feel they really have learnt something, or have been entertained, or that this time they will do something about the problem. If the audience reacts in the way the speaker hopes, then the speaker has made a successful speech.

POINTS TO REMEMBER

Be natural. Don't attempt to dress up your speech in language you are not accustomed to using. Don't try to make yourself sound like a prominent politician. Don't try to 'act' just because people are looking at you.

Speak as clearly as you can. Try not to mumble or gabble your words. Take a little time to get each thought clear in your mind before you begin each sentence. Try to say all you have to say on one point before you start on the next.

Don't worry about being nervous—worrying will make you more nervous. There will be many in the audience who will remember their first attempt at public speaking and they will here you out sympathetically and with interest if you have something worthwhile to say.

A good speech is one that is a happy blending of the speaker and their speech. Show your personal involvement.

If your listeners can tell from your manner as well as from your words that what you are saying is what you really believe, they will sit back and listen with a great deal of interest. If you show your enthusiasm and your personal involvement in the subject they will respond accordingly. Enthusiasm is catching. You, and your speech, could start something far greater than you ever imagined.

PART 1: SPEAKING IN PUBLIC

MAKING A START

Your first step is to start thinking before the occasion. Think about what you intend to say to the meeting. Jot down ideas as they come to you. Make a list of all the things that have influenced you in reaching your decision. If necessary, get in touch with officials to check facts and figures.

When you have decided what you are going to say, decide the purpose of your speech, because not until then can you decide what material you should use and how it should be arranged.

For example, suppose that you regularly attend the parents and teachers meetings of the local school, and that at the next meeting they will be discussing a proposal to raise $5,000 to build and equip a school library. You've got definite views on the matter and so you should plan a speech in which to express these.

We will assume that you believe the meeting should not make a decision on the library project until more precise information has been made available to parents. Your problem, then, is to present your remarks in such a fashion that others will also realise the need for more details. In other words, your job as a speaker is to convince or persuade the meeting to accept your point of view.

Keeping this in mind, arrange the points you have jotted down so that they will have a cumulative effect on your listeners.

Provided you are not the only person who needs more information, you will find some of your audience nodding in agreement if you speak of 'others in the same boat.' Thus you will be in the happy position of having at least some of the audience on your side right from the start.

If you don't clutter up your sentences with a lot of words, everyone will understand what you mean. Use words that are typically 'you,' in your own style; natural, simple, direct, and sensible. Even slightly 'slangy' phrases are preferable to pretentious expressions.

A good way to finish is with a closing sentence which will bring a few chuckles before the applause. Be careful not to offend anybody or come down heavily on officials for not providing all the answers long ago. If your manner is friendly throughout, the purpose of your speech to convince the meeting that to proceed without more information would be leaping in the dark— will be obvious to all.

Suppose that you oppose the plan—that you are fed up with the long, drawn-out discussions and that you believe there are more urgent matters to be dealt with. How would you go about preparing your speech?

First, do your thinking very carefully. What will you achieve if you rubbish the library project? How much support are you likely to get if you want the idea dropped? Are there urgent matters which should be dealt with or is this just your idea of things?

Keep calm. You should never make your first speech on a topic which is likely to make you hot under the collar. It's too easy to lose control of yourself and perhaps say things which later you will regret. So, discipline your thinking and eliminate anything that sounds like a personal attack or an invitation to violent disagreement. Set down carefully each point you want to make. Try to decide on the best words to use and, under each point, write a phrase or two to help you remember them. Be prepared to stick to what you have in your notes so that there is no chance of your flying off the handle.

HOW TO INSPIRE PEOPLE TO ACTION

For the sake of this exercise we'll imagine that you want to have the library project dropped in favour of providing adequate shelter for the children. To do this, you will need to do more than convince or persuade. You'll need to arouse the meeting and get them to realise the urgency of the problem so that they will take action.

A pretty blunt speech which gets to the heart of the matter in a very few words something that many well-known speakers fail to do—should be most effective.

It will be one which doesn't pull any punches, but at the same time avoids being rude or insulting. Put everyone on the spot. They will have to make a decision for themselves 'do you reckon that books are more important than health?'

A good device is to make the closing sentence virtually a repeat of the opening one, making quite clear in the two most important parts of your speech (the opening and the conclusion) what you want done. Throw down the gauntlet and the audience will have to accept your challenge.

PREPARING A SPEECH

Let us assume that you have a better than average stamp collection and, because of this, you have been invited to talk on 'stamp collecting.'

Your first essential step is to find out all you can about your audience.

As has been said before, the whole purpose of a speech should be to give something of value to your listeners. If you don't stop to think about your audience, how can you hope to give them something worthwhile? Here are the questions you should try to find answers to:

1. What is the age group of your audience?
2. Will the audience be men or women?
3. Approximately how many people will you have to speak to?
4. What is their educational or professional level?
5. Is the group affiliated with any organisation—religious, political, educational, charitable, etc.?
6. Have they any specific interests: child welfare, pensioners, Red Cross, etc.?
7. What aspect of your subject are they most likely to be interested in?

These are pretty obvious questions, yet it is surprising how often experienced speakers ignore them. Let's see how different answers determine the type of speech most likely to be well-received.

Example 1: The group consists of mostly men, from thirty-five to seventy; about half are accountants, lawyers, doctors, teachers; they are a non-political, non-religious group whose main object is to preserve the natural beauty of their locality. Usual attendance between forty and fifty.

Speech possibilities: Stamp collecting as an investment

Historic buildings portrayed on stamps.

Rare and unusual stamps.

Famous gardens, plants, and animals.

Example 2: The group consists of men and women of all ages and walks of life; they belong to a church and raise money for good causes not necessarily connected with their church.

Speech possibilities: The educational value in stamp collecting.

Religion on stamps.

Used stamps are valuable.

Interesting stories about certain stamps.

The work of the Red Cross on stamps.

Example 3: The group consists of men and women; all over sixty; a good number are pensioners; they meet once a month for entertainment and fellowship. The meeting is sponsored by the local council. At least fifty people attend.

Speech possibilities: Reminiscing with stamps.

A trip around the world.

From windjammers to the space age.

Historic buildings or famous places.

Great events during the lifetime of the audience, pictured on stamps.

Now that you have considered the possible interests of your audience, your next step is to consider the following:

1. Your own preference.
2. The occasion.
3. Length and timing of the speech.
4. Advance preparation.
5. Research.

1. YOUR OWN PREFERENCE COMPARED TO THE AUDIENCE

Your biggest problem will probably be to reconcile what you would like to speak about and what you feel your audience would prefer to hear. You may be a specialist in one aspect of a subject, but, if you have done your preliminary investigation thoroughly, you will be foolish to speak on it if the audience would not be capable of understanding, or interested in following your remarks.

2. THE OCCASION

For example, is it going to be a formal occasion? Are you the only speaker? Will you speak after a meal with the audience still at the tables? If there is to be more than one speaker, who are the other speakers? What are their subjects? What is the order of speaking? Will you be speaking in a strange hall? Will you have to use a microphone?

It is essential for you to know all this so that you will not find yourself at a disadvantage. For example, you may he the last of three speakers, each speaking for, perhaps 10-12 minutes. If the first two give light-hearted speeches, your serious speech may suffer. It could be even worse if the first two speeches have been rather heavy going. By the time you get to your feet most of the audience would appreciate something light and amusing.

Of course it isn't always possible to know in advance what other speakers will do, but it is worth making the effort to find out what they are likely to do before you get down to the job of preparing your material.

3. LENGTH AND TIMING OF THE SPEECH

The amount of time you have been allowed will determine how much you can say. A man who knows his subject can talk on it for hours and some speakers do this, to the infinite boredom of their listeners. Don't attempt to cover a lot of ground very quickly. It is far better to restrict yourself to what can comfortably be covered in the time allotted to you, making sure that your audience will have time to appreciate and understand what you say to them as you go along.

Advance preparation. Don't leave your preparation to the last minute. You may find that something that you wanted to mention needs checking and the material is not available. A certain amount of research is required for most speeches and, if it isn't possible to verify points in time, it's far better to leave that part out than to say something which may not be accurate.

Having completed the preliminaries, you now have to decide the exact purpose of your speech, and you'll be in a much better position to make the decision once you have all the facts about the audience and the occasion before you.

4. RESEARCH

Only then should you start your research. If you do it this way you will save yourself a lot of time and effort by being able to concentrate your search for that which you know you can use. Make full use of libraries (and their research services) and of newspaper files as well as consulting specific organisations. But avoid trying to cram your memory with all the information contained in large volumes.

Finally, we come to arranging the material in the best possible way to achieve the purpose of the speech.

To do this we must first study the elements of a speech.

THE ELEMENTS OF A SPEECH

THE NATURE OF A SPEECH

A good speech is a carefully planned form of expression. And, in the planning of it, you must constantly remember that a speech is something to be heard. It makes its first impression on the ears of an audience. For this reason, the sound of a speech is just as important as its literary form. A speech like a poem, should have a latent beauty, power, appeal, or emotion of any kind which needs only the voice of the speaker to bring it to life.

It is not easy to prepare the spoken word. We are so accustomed to reading that we forget that the voice cannot speak as quickly as the eye can read. The eye records the layout of the paragraphs and notes words in italics, quotations, parentheses, and so on. The brain instantly conditions the reader for the introduction of new material, the devices of the writer.

But how are you—the speaker—going to get your message across to the whole audience which can use only ears, not eyes? How will they know what you are quoting or when you've come to the end of a paragraph and start to introduce some new material?

Think on these points as we look at the anatomy of a speech and remember that the examples you will use should appeal more to the ear than the eye. We will discuss the sound of a speech later.

THE FORM OF A SPEECH

Divide your speech into three parts:

- The opening
- The body or development
- The conclusion

Unfortunately, a lot of people have the idea that there's a sort of fence between each section, and they build speeches accordingly, with the result that the audience can almost see the fence dividing the body of the speech from the conclusion.

A speech is a whole thing and must be prepared that way. It is completely wrong to think in terms of a speech being in parts, except for the purpose of analysis.

THE OPENING

Interest

There is always one thing you should try to do—attract the interest of your audience right from the start. If you can't get their attention in the first couple of minutes, they may lose interest altogether.

Your speech should have a definite purpose and the type of opening should depend on what you hope to achieve from the whole speech. Let's have a look at some different types of speeches and consider what sort of opening you should use.

A speech which sets out to inform or instruct

Be brief! When there isn't enough time to deal fully with your subject, say so early in your speech. When you have to define or explain, do so briefly and simply. Don't waste time telling what you will not be talking about.

Avoid confusing references: Don't begin by referring to something recently reported in the papers or on television. If people have read the article, you're not telling them anything new. If they haven't read it, or seen the TV follow-up, you will have some of your listeners at an immediate disadvantage. By all means refer to what has been reported, but do it at a later stage in your speech when your listeners will have had a chance to understand what your purpose is.

Try to have an individual approach: Whenever you plan an opening, try to get away from the routine approach. Be imaginative.

Try an opening that doesn't set out to dazzle the audience with brilliant words. Let it be a very simple indication of your intention. There's nothing actually wrong with an opening which puts all your cards on the table—it's just bad psychology. It is better to keep the audience guessing, playing one card at a time as your speech progresses. Curiosity keeps an audience alive—and awake.

A speech which sets out to convince or persuade

You might choose an intriguing title for your speech. Most people will think they know what the speech is about but they won't be absolutely sure for a while. So put some imagination into your titles. 'The First IC' looks and sounds more intriguing than 'Reading is Rewarding,' even though the latter may be the tenor of your remarks.

Use a light touch: Before you set out to convince or persuade, consider what opposition your speech may generate. If you try to ram your ideas down your listeners' throats, you may get your fingers bitten. To be persuasive try a light touch, a little humour, and make it clear that you understand the opposite point of view.

Do not talk at your audience, even chiding them. Avoid dogmatic or contentious remarks early in the speech which may alienate quite a number of people and make the task of persuading or convincing much more difficult.

Use an anecdote or story: This opening provides an approach to the subject which is quite casual. If you narrate some little scene convincingly you should be rewarded with a few smiles and chuckles. The audience will relax because your beginning has been friendly, informal, and unexpected. They will be more open to suggestion because you have already established that vital link between speaker and audience, without which no speech is ever successful.

The bold approach: If you are a competent speaker and have the ability to cope with the unexpected, try a bolder approach but don't try a flippant style unless you can sustain it. You must be confident that you can capitalize on any audience reaction, which means that you must know your subject extremely well and have a ready answer for any situation. It also means that you may have to re-arrange your material and perhaps omit or gloss over some parts and develop others more extensively than you had planned. In other words, you are going to let the audience call the tune. This is dangerous ground for novices.

A speech which sets out to arouse people to action

Imagine that you believe strongly that parents should do more to prevent accidents in the home; that you have statistics and authoritative opinions to support your case, and that the purpose of your speech is to enroll members into a 'Safer Homes Campaign.'

Use of statistics: How will you begin? Don't start by quoting a lot of figures. If you want to introduce statistics at any stage in the speech, keep them in simple form.

For example: 'Last year the City Hospital treated an average of five children a day for injuries received at home. Think about that for a moment. Five children a day, every day for 365 days. That's nearly 2,000 suffering children. No one knows how many minor cases were treated at home or in doctors' rooms. Probably 10,000. The tragedy is that a high percentage of injuries could have been prevented if parents realised there's no place like home—for accidents.

The 'Safer Homes campaign' is . . . .

'Five a day' is easy to remember. It's also easy for the audience to miss, so it is repeated in a way in which its impact cannot fail to register: 'five children a day, every day for 365 days.' The round figures (2,000 and 10,000) will stick in the mind without any effort for a long time to come.

Note that the point is made very early that parents could have prevented many of the accidents if …, and the 'Safer Homes Campaign' follows immediately.

Dramatic opening: You may prefer to use a 'shock' opening: 'A little girl of five is dead, after months of suffering, because her mother kept the caustic soda on the bottom shelf. A toddler of two will never walk without a limp. His father backed the car over him. Have you seen what a pan of fat can do to the face and body of a child … ?'

Perhaps a 'dramatic' opening appeals to you – a mother 'on trial' because of her negligence, or a description of a life-saving operation?

'Shock' and 'dramatic' openings can be very effective when done well, but you should first consider whether you need to jolt your audience so severely right at the start. If you want people to sign on the dot ted line, don't spend too much time on scenes of suffering and sorrow. Highlight , the 'Campaign,' not the broken bodies. Give yourself time to explain how the 'Campaign' works. Keep underlining the responsibilities of the parents and the help they will get from being 'Campaigners.'

A speech which sets out to entertain or amuse

A lot of amusing after-dinner speakers don't really make speeches at all. They simply present to a relaxed and ready-to-be-amused audience a string of jokes, funny stories, or ludicrous situations which, if told in austere surroundings, would scarcely raise a smile.

A humorous speech requires just as much preparation as a serious speech. One thing that marks a successful humorous speaker is his ability to produce something original, unusual, or completely unexpected.

Sometimes the title is like the launching pad of a space craft. Once launched, the speaker gets further and further away from it. Every now and then he pretends to get back to the subject, only to veer away again on to some subject almost completely divorced from the topic. This twisting and turning can be highly amusing and, because the audience has no idea what is coming next, curiosity and interest keep them wide awake.

Naturally, you could begin with a funny story (provided it is funny). Or you could develop a crazy situation, so long as the audience doesn't have to wait too long for a laugh. Whatever you decide to do, remember that one laugh won't make you known as a witty speaker. The pot must be kept bubbling all the time.

Speeches in general

Be selective: Suppose you want to make a speech on Charles Dickens. Is it the man or his works you want to talk about? In a speech of less than 15 minutes you can't do both. If you decide to talk about the man, don't give his life chronologically. It will sound too much like an obituary. Begin at some interesting or important point in his career and 'flash back' to those dates, places, or incidents that are necessary.

Use quotations: If you intend to speak about the stories Dickens wrote, a quotation would make an effective opening. But don't make it long, and do try to memorise it. If you read it, the audience may get the impression that you are going to read all your speech, and that's not an exciting prospect.

Use words with care: Sometimes it is necessary (or desirable) to create an atmosphere right at the start. You should carefully consider every word—not just its meaning; its sound, too, is vitally important. Male audiences have a habit of putting the wrong interpretation on some words, especially during after-dinner speeches.

The rhetorical question
This is a conventional opening gambit. To do this effectively the questions should be related so that their effect is either progressive or cumulative. Don't clutter up a question with a lot of commentary. Let it stand out, bold and well-defined, so that there is no doubt about what you are asking. Then pause for a second or two to let it sink in.

THE BODY (OR DEVELOPMENT) OF A SPEECH
When you start planning the body of your speech, keep in mind its overall plan and intention. The significant thing is to keep the speech moving towards its destination.

If, for example, you are giving a speech on 'historic landmarks . . . ,' say all you have to say about one place before going on to the next. If you keep skipping from place to place you'll confuse your listeners.

Give some thought to the sequence of places. Remember, you don't have to start at the begining. It might be better to work your way to the place where it all started. Perhaps one of the places has been in the news lately. If so, start there, because it's topical.

Don't get carried away with information on one place so that you have to skip through the last one or two because you have run out of time.

Unity: Any speech which is basically a presentation of a number of items should have a continuity of feeling and purpose that runs like a silken thread through the fabric of the whole speech.

A speech to convince or persuade

There are special requirements when you set out to convince or persuade an audience.

Be logical: Your reasoning must be sound and your evidence clearly presented, and there should be a flow or development of ideas that is either logical or natural. Without these, your conclusions may not be acceptable to your listeners.

Avoid vague generalizations: You can't hope to convince an audience by making arbitrary distinctions such as 'the world could easily be divided into three groups those who can't read, those who only read what they have to, and those who enjoy reading.' This is such a debatable foundation that any edifice you build on it could be easily shaken down.

Be aware of other points of view: Imagine what the opposition would do to some of your arguments if you were speaking in a debate. Even though your audience will have to sit in silence, you can't stop them debating mentally what you are saying, and, if they can pick holes in your case, how can you convince them?

Quotations: Unless you intend to present only your own views and experiences you should buttress your statements with brief quotations from recognized authorities.

Above all, plan: Choose your words with care. Check your facts. Don't make long-winded explanations. Use imagination in the way you present your case. Plan your speech so that it gradually builds up to a climax.

A speech to get action

In this kind of speech you can usually draw on your own knowledge and experience so that there is no difficulty in getting material. The greatest problem is deciding what to leave out. If you have made an investigation of the group you are to speak to you'll he able to make the right decision.

Use the personal approach: It's a good idea to begin with a personal experience. It tells the audience something about you. They can get some idea of your point of view and gauge your involvement in the subject. Your aim then is to get them to accept your attitude so that you can more easily arouse them to do whatever you have in mind.

Don't attempt a style of language that is not natural to you. Don't try to act a dramatic part. Sincerity and enthusiasm are required.

Use illustrations: The Chinese have a saying 'A picture is worth ten thousand words.' Remember this. If you can quickly get your audience to see what you are talking about, instead of having to listen intently to many words of explanation or illustration, they will react more spontaneously and your objective more easily achieved.

But do use illustrations which can clearly be seen by all present. If you want to use a chart, map, or graph (and these can be very useful), make sure that the lettering is large enough to be read by all the audience. Make sure that there is a suitable stand available for displaying your charts. Be careful that when you point out features you continue to talk with your back to the listeners. Your explanations may be lost if you do.

An entertaining speech

Comedy is a serious business. It calls for the greatest attention to the smallest detail; you must constantly search for the right word and the right phrase. Not necessarily right in a literary or grammatical sense, but right for the purpose of the speaker.

Because your main purpose is to entertain or to amuse, you must try to anticipate how the audience will react. If some of your jokes fall flat, the fault may be yours, not theirs. On the other hand, it can be very disconcerting if your listeners laugh unexpectedly. Maybe you used a word you didn't mean to. Or the mention of a name or place triggered the audience into laughter at some private or local joke which you were quite unprepared for.

Try the unexpected: A logical development of ideas or a natural sequence of events is not important. Often it is the very illogical and ridiculous arguments and arrangement of material that make a speech so funny. But, if you present a series of separate episodes or stories, there needs to be some link between them.

Observe good taste: Good humour should never offend or even run the risk of offending. Don't make fun of religious beliefs. Even caricatures of people should be drawn with an eye to the reaction of the audience. You may laugh at people, but if you give the impression that you are ridiculing them, you may become offensive.

Common faults in humorous speeches:
1. Too many un-funny words which don't hold the speech together.
2. The use of stale jokes and stories that have done the rounds.
3. The laborious development of situations which aren't particularly amusing after all.
4. Poor characterization and the inability to sustain the character throughout the speech.
5. Laughter from the speaker before he delivers the punch line.
6. Moving on to the next joke before the audience has finished laughing at the first.
7. The use of 'blue' jokes or material which is in questionable taste.

THE CONCLUSION

It would be stupid for a speaker not to prepare their conclusion and to present it spontaneously.

This is the part of your speech which gives the audience their last look at the subject, or brings the whole thing to a purposeful climax. It should leave them with a lasting impression, or a clear and undistorted picture in their minds. In this vital segment nothing should be left to chance. Hesitancy or mumbled words could spoil what had been up until then an absorbing speech.

In some types of speech (those to instruct and persuade) it is a good idea to use the last few minutes for a recapitulation or summing-up. Very briefly review the highlights (use as few words as possible) and then put forward what you want your audience to keep in their minds.

When your speech has been clearly divided into sections, (e.g. 'Historic Landmarks' where you discuss first one place, then another) make sure that your ending relates to the whole speech, not just to the part previously dealt with. (This is a common fault in this type of speech.)

Use of questions
Frequently the closing section begins with a question for example:

1. *'Will you enrol as a member of the 'Safer Homes Campaign'?'*
If you have already explained the 'Safer Homes Campaign' and what it hopes to achieve, this type of ending is good. For the remainder of your time you should continue to put the pressure on your audience by using more questions: 'Will you continue to leave those tablets and mixtures within easy reach of your children? Or that bottle of cleaning fluid behind the door in the laundry?' And so on.

2. *'How is this likely to affect us in the next 20 years?'*
This example is not good. How can you expect to answer that question satisfactorily in your last 2 or 3 minutes? If you don't attempt to answer it, your audience may feel let-down, because they would certainly want to know. You should, instead, have eliminated some of the build-up so that the question came about the half-way mark. Your ending could have been that we had better make up our minds before it is too late, or, that we should start now to adapt ourselves for the change which must inevitably come soon.

Use of humour

For after-dinner speeches, save something really amusing for the end. If you are telling a tale, and your whole speech is virtually a story, make sure that the ending isn't obvious long before you get to it. Have something unexpected up your sleeve. Don't finish with a funny story just because it is a funny story. Use it only if it fits into the pattern of the whole speech.

Use of quotations

Probably everybody knows that a good way to end is to use a quotation. The quotation should not be lengthy. Check for accuracy. ('Money is the root of all evil' is probably the most misquoted quotation and has quite a different meaning from that of the original.) Learn your quotation so that you are word-perfect. Many speakers put themselves in a bad light when they say 'If we applied those well-known words . . .' and then read the well-known words from their notes. Don't use a quotation if it doesn't adequately sum up, or reflect the tenor of the entire speech.

SOME DON'TS

Don't stop abruptly, catching everyone by surprise.

Don't have false endings. Some speakers give every sign of stopping, but start off again and repeat the process several times before sitting down.

Don't fail to have an ending. There are those who just stop talking about their subject, and, sometimes in mid-sentence say '. . . Well, I think that's all I can say on the subject.'

Don't assume too much. Many speakers say something like this—'I'm sure that you will all agree with me that ...' How can you hope that all will agree? Probably half the audience will be waiting to debate points with you after the meeting. This too-confident type of ending hardly achieves anything—except to bring the speech to a close.

Don't refer too confidently to the proof of 'facts.' Have you really presented facts? Or have they been your own opinions? Even facts supported by authorities can be countered by opposing experts. (Consider the conflict of opinion on fluoridation).

Don't make your closing section obvious by 'sign-posting' it —'in conclusion may I say . . .' Or 'finally, let me sum up the situation.'

Don't say 'thank you' at the end. It's the audience who should do this.

THE SOUND OF A SPEECH

A famous person once said: 'Three things matter in a speech. Who says it, how he says it, and what he says, and, of the three, the last matters the least.'

At first sight this may seem a gross exaggeration, but think for a moment . .. . How often have you been bored by bishops, put to sleep by politicians, or left behind by lecturers—although they were experts on their subjects? What they said meant nothing to you, simply because you didn't enjoy listening to them. Why?

IMPORTANCE OF VOICE

In speech-making, the voice and the words must complement one another. How can a speaker make his audience enthuse over his ideas if his voice is dull and dreary, or his manner aloof or indifferent? What's the use of a speaker raising his voice and thumping the table if there is nothing of substance in his words?

Too frequently speakers fail to get the most out of a sentence because they use emphasis indiscriminately. It's not always the obvious word that should be stressed. A good illustration is provided in the familiar words: 'The Lord is my shepherd; I shall not want.' Probably ninety-nine out of 100 people would read or speak these words like this: 'The **Lord** is my shepherd; I **shall** not **want**.' (Slight emphasis on bold words.)

If you experiment with these few words, shifting the emphasis, enlarging a key word slightly, and varying the speed of delivery, you will discover that the listener can be presented with different meanings. The original is not lost, but something has been added to it.

Many sentences contain one or more words which are more important than the rest, and the speaker indicates their importance by emphasizing them. Generally this is done by speaking the words more loudly. You can, at the same time, draw a word out a little. For example, if you want to emphasize the word 'large' in this sentence: 'It is a very large country'you would make it sound like this 'It is a very LA-ARGE country.'

There are times when several consecutive words could well be emphasized, as in the sentence 'It is a VERY LARGE COUNTRY.' There are other times when more than one word is important, but not equally so. Consequently, emphasis must be subtle. It must not be used mechanically.

PAUSING

Nothing speaks louder than silence and the well-placed pause is just as effective as the appropriate emphasis. It has additional advantages that can help you to enslave your audience.

If you've got truth and conviction on your side you can make an audience squirm after a painful accusation '. . . and the fault lies HERE (short pause). . . RIGHT IN THIS ROOM (much longer pause.)'

You can also surprise an audience by slipping in something quite unexpected after a silence. The pause helps to build suspense. Instead of pressing on to the climax, pause a little, and have your listeners sitting on the edges of their chairs waiting for what comes next. If you avoid long sentences it will help.

PRONUNCIATION

While on the subject of words, cultivate the habit of checking pronunciation. You will often hear a person described as 'hosPITable. Occasionally you hear the word pronounced 'hOSpitable.' Which is correct?

It's surprising how many words we mispronounce. Try yourself out on the following and check with a dictionary:

apparatus
adult
controversy
deficit
despicable
finance
irrevocable
municipal
penalize
robust

COMMON DIFFICULTIES

Some people are lucky and have voices which are easy to listen to. Others tend to speak nasally, or their voices are a trifle shrill. Some speak clearly and distinctly, others mumble or run the end of one word into the next (a typical Australian failing). Some speak so rapidly that it's exhausting trying to keep up with them. Others take so long to say anything that it's hard for the audience to concentrate.

Which category do you fit into? Have you ever listened critically to your voice? You should, if you want to be a successful speaker. Get a tape-recorder and let it record your voice in many moods reading, talking to friends, arguing, recounting the affairs of the day not just for a few minutes, but for half an hour or more. Then sit back and listen to yourself. After the first shock of hearing the sound of your own voice as others hear it, listen to the way you speak and remember that this is what an audience has to put up with.

A MONOTONOUS TONE

Don't maintain a constant tonal level from start to finish. If your speech ranges from funerals to fun parlours, lovers to lunatics, or surfing to slavery, you must vary the sound of your words. Otherwise the speech will have no life in it, no light and shade, no feeling. It will be as sleep- inducing as the buzz of a bee on a warm day.

Your voice is an instrument with a wide range of sounds capable of expressing every mood. Use the high notes and the low notes. To help you to appreciate the possibilities of interpretation read and record a couple of paragraphs in your normal speaking voice. Then record it again several times, each time expressing a different mood or feeling. You'll be surprised how different each will sound.

An audience can easily become bored or irritated if your voice follows a regular tonal or rhythmic pattern. If you begin each sentence on the same note, go up the scale a bit, and then, as the sentence ends, come down again, the effect is soporific. Usually, with this downward curve, the voice grows softer, too. Sometimes the last few words are spoken so quietly and pitched so low that only those in the front row could possibly hear them.

Many who offend this way don't realise how consistently they drop their voices as they come to the end of a sentence. Nor are they aware that every time they ask a question (in a speech) they do the same thing.

A question (as well as other important sentences) will have far more impact if the voice moves in an upward curve. Try it on the tape-recorder and notice the difference.

Some speakers are like leaky taps. Their words drip out with a steady, monotonous beat—some fast, some slow, some at an easy pace. But the evenness of delivery makes a listener feel like planting a bomb under the speaker to see if it will shake him. And yet, off the platform these speakers can be as animated in conversation as anyone.

DISJOINTED SENTENCES

Unfortunately many speakers make little pauses (more properly 'breaks') all over the place. 'with the result (break) that the sentence they (break) are constructing (break) sounds (break) something like an old-fashioned (break) gramo phone (break) playing a cracked (break) record.'

Nervousness causes some of this. Lack of preparation may also be part of the trouble. Sometimes it has become a habit which the speaker isn't conscious of. The listener finds this type of speaker one of the hardest to listen to. It sounds as though he were making it up as he went along.

If you detect these meaningless breaks on your tape-recording you must immediately take steps to break the habit before it breaks you. Try deliberately and conscientiously to deliver a complete sentence.

NERVOUSNESS

A speaker who is very nervous concentrates so hard on what they have to say that they are not able to think about how they should be saying it. They know they are nervous. They realise that the audience will probably discover this too, although, generally speaking, it's not nearly as obvious as they imagine.

Because of their determination to get the words out, they don't listen to himself. The steady, measured tone may result from an iron discipline. They keep telling themselves not to panic. They know they will gabble their words or speak too quickly if they lose control. They never realise that in avoiding one error, they are committing a greater one.

The flat, level tone could result from a lack of self-confidence.

The dropping of the voice at the end of sentences probably began with their need to keep checking the script. When the novice speaker looks down at his notes as he or she is talking, they invariably bends their head, projecting the voice towards the floor and constricting the vocal passages, with the result that the voice sounds lower and softer.

Confidence will enable a speaker (provided they have prepared their material thoroughly) to listen to the sound of their voice rather than to concentrate on expressing himself.

YOUR APPEARANCE

Never forget that the audience uses eyes as well as ears. If people don't like what they see, they may not bother to listen.

If you have to sit in full view of the audience, remember that you will be subjected to more than a casual examination by those who are to listen to you later. If it appears that you are bored by the preliminaries, the audience may be slow to respond to you. Don't move about in your seat (even if it is uncomfortable). Don't fiddle with your clothes or your notes. The audience may interpret these movements as signs of nervousness, which won't make them eager to hear you.

When you have been introduced, don't stand at the lectern or table shuffling your notes, jingling the coins in your pocket, or polishing your glasses. Make no last-minute adjustments to your hair or your tie. Don't lean on the lectern or prop yourself against the table.

All your movements should be controlled but relaxed, so that the audience will feel that you are free from tension, nervousness, or indifference.

When you are ready to begin, wait until there is complete silence before saying a word.

STANCE

It doesn't really matter how you stand provided that the audience is not distracted. A speaker who never moves cannot expect to arouse any great feeling. Neither can the speaker who tends to wander about the stage.

Your stance should be comfortable, both for you and the audience. And comfort implies a naturalness of position. An exaggerated posture will make the audience feel scarcely more comfortable than the speaker looks. Beware of any sort of rocking motion, whether a heel and toe movement, stepping, or swaying. Ladies should be particularly careful if they balance on heel and toe. Some of the male audience may be more interested in the balancing act than in the speech.

HANDS

Hands are a real problem for the novice speaker. For some reason he becomes very conscious of his hands. Every now and then he puts them behind his back, then into his pockets, or locks them in prayerful gesture, or holds grimly on to the table or lectern. If he doesn't do something with his hands they flap about like the broken arms of a windmill.

If you use notes it gives your hands something to do—occasionally changing them from one hand to the other. (There will be more about notes later.)

Once you've done a bit of public speaking and gained confidence, the problem of what to do with your hands will soon disappear.

GESTURES

A gesture should be an extension of your speech and not a physical movement unrelated to it. The golden rule is—don't use gestures unless they add something of value to your speech.

The obvious gesture is a waste of energy; the repetitive gesture loses its value, and anything exaggerated or dramatic (unless skilfully done and appropriate to the words) may give the audience a bit of a giggle. ('You should have seen the way he carried on when he talked about . . .')

In the early stages, you should plan and rehearse your gestures. As you gain confidence and experience you will find that they will soon become involuntary, arising from your total involvement in what you are saying.

USING NOTES

There is no shame attached to the use of notes. In fact, there are many good reasons why notes are an advantage. Apart from giving your hands something to do, they enable you to refer to important sections of your speech where a lapse of memory would be disastrous. They will also ensure that you keep to your planned sequence of ideas.

Notes should never be large—about A4 is a handy size. They should be tidy, legible, and on fairly stiff paper. No speaker should ever apologize because he mis-read his notes.

Don't use notes that are so small that you turn them over at the rate of one a minute. After a while you look like a card dealer. Don't start without them if there is any doubt that you will want them, because it is an embarrassing moment for all when you begin to flounder, then reach into your pocket and have to thumb through your notes to find what you need.

Similarly, keep your notes up with your speech, even if you only refer to them occasionally.

Don't put your notes on the table. If you do, you will bend down to read them and your voice will be lost. Don't try to hide your notes at your side or behind your back and then sneak a quick look at them when you need to. Always keep your notes in a handy position so that you can raise them to about chest height when you want them. If you do this, you can glance down without lowering your head more than a fraction.

USE YOUR EYES

Watch your audience. It won't be long before you can read them like a book. If they aren't looking at you, they're probably not listening. Or they may be listening but without interest.

Don't gaze at one particular spot or one section of the audience. Don't look at their feet or over their heads. You can't afford to ignore any section of your audience, so you must learn to look at them all. But don't make the turning of your head a mechanical movement.

People make contact in many different ways and even the fleeting moment when a speaker looks right into the eyes of a person can be rewarding and revealing.

MANNER

Apart from the dead-pan humorist, no speaker can afford to keep his face devoid of expression. Most of us never have the chance to see ourselves as others see us, so we need the help of a kind but honest critic.

Discover any habits which may distract the audience —frowning, head on one side, running the tongue over the lips, etc.

A speaker needs to show animation and feeling in his face but there must be no hint of affectation. Facial expression should be the outward appearance of your inner feelings. If you feel like smiling, smile but don't 'say cheese.'

THE USE OF WORDS

If you want to be a good public speaker you should make a study of words.

REFERENCE GUIDES

You will need three different kinds of references:

1. A dictionary, for correct meanings and pronunciations;
2. A guide to the proper use of words;
3. A Thesaurus, 'a storehouse of knowledge.'

Don't start finding excuses for delaying. If you devoted only 10 minutes each day to improving your vocabulary it would be worth it. If you checked the meaning and pronunciation of only one word each day, or discovered one new word and learnt how to use it, it would make a considerable difference to your vocabulary.

Unfortunately, many people 'build' their speeches by reaching into a stack of words in their vocabulary and taking the first one, without stopping to realise that words have strength, movement, colour, feeling, rhythm, and so on, and that it is very hard to find one word that will exactly take the place of another word. If you've never thought of this before, consider the following:

The following report appeared in a newspaper: 'In one raid North Vietnamese troops killed 16 villagers who refused to betray their chief.'

Commenting on the attack, a United States spokesman was quoted as saying 'The victims were assassinated gunned down in cold blood.'

This is a good example of the power of words. The first account is factual and unemotional. It scarcely registers on the mind as you sip your morning coffee. The second statement carries with it overtones of horror, hatred, and cruelty, yet the basic facts have not been changed.

It's not a question of one report being right and the other wrong after all, sixteen villagers were killed (or assassinated). It's a matter of the purpose behind the words.

Once you realise how important the subtleties of the English language can be to anyone who wants to influence others, you'll never think of words as 'bricks and mortar' again, and you will examine your vocabulary with new interest.

For example, do you make a habit of using words like 'dreadful', 'amazing', 'colossal', 'nice'? If you do, it's a safe bet that you are just using them to plug gaps in sentences.

And what about those absurd combinations 'awfully nice', 'terribly sweet', and so on?

When you stop to think about them they are ridiculous.

CLICHÉS

Try to avoid clichés which are so old that they have lost all appeal. Similes, metaphors, and descriptive phrases are the life-blood of good speeches but they lose their effectiveness with over-use. Why do we always 'explore every avenue' and 'leave no stone unturned'? 'Far be it for me' to work while the Government, 'in its wisdom', declares that, 'by and large', it has the situation 'well in hand.'

Cicero is reputed to have said: 'The public speaker must set forth with power and attractiveness the very same topic which others discuss in such tame and bloodless phraseology.'

RESPECT SIMPLICITY

Whatever you do, do not be misled into thinking that language for public speaking needs to be dressed up. Some of the finest speeches the world has ever known have been remembered for generations because the simplicity of the words and the clarity of expression have kept the meaning and purpose of the speech alive. Do not despise the one-syllable word.

POINTS TO REMEMBER WHEN SPEAKING

1. *Thinking* should always precede the preparation of a speech.

2. Make *notes* of thoughts as they occur to you.

3. Remember the *purpose* of your speech when preparing it.

4. From your notes, write out your thoughts in the *order* best calculated to achieve your purpose.

5. Use your own *style* of words and phrases—but you should try to eliminate any bad habits of language, grammar, or diction.

6. Avoid *long sentences*. Short sentences will help you to be more easily understood and to prevent you from making grammatical errors.

7. When the chair calls on you to speak, don't say a word until the audience is *quiet* and attentive.

8. *Look* at your audience when you speak.

9. Speak *calmly*—not too quickly or too slowly. Make sure that all members of the audience can hear you.

10. Use *notes*. Far better to use them and refer to them than to forget part of your speech.

11. Be confident and *enthusiastic*. You will probably be nervous, but there's no need to advertise the fact by shuffling your feet, fiddling with your clothes, or waving your hands about.

12. Make a speech *whenever you can*. Get to your feet and practise public speaking whenever you have something to say that is worth listening to. Never get up just for the sake of talking. There are already far too many people who love the sound of their own voices.

13. This last point may be corny, but it's good advice for any speaker
Stand up to be seen.
Speak up to be heard.
Shut up to be appreciated.

FORMAL SPEECHES

One day you will be asked to move a vote of thanks, propose a toast, introduce a guest speaker, or perform one of those speaking tasks which are a necessary part of many functions. Unfortunately, these tasks are allotted for reasons quite divorced from your ability to speak in public. If you are president of a group you will have to present reports and welcome visitors; if you're the bride- groom or best man you'll have to propose a toast; if you have a special connection with a guest , speaker, you are sure to be asked either to introduce him or to move a vote of thanks.

The first thing you must decide is whether your task is a personal one or whether your are the spokesman for a group. (Example: an introduction may be largely personal but a welcome should not be, because the welcome should come from those assembled, through their chosen speaker.)

OCCASION

Weddings involve mainly friends and relations, and speeches are therefore more free-and-easy, with personal anecdotes and family jokes quite acceptable to the majority. Some meetings and gatherings are much more formal. This does not mean that humour is out of place. It does mean that chatty speeches or a series of intimate personal snippets are inappropriate.

Take into account local customs and traditions. This doesn't mean that you should slavishly follow the well-worn path, but you are advised to consider carefully the reaction of the assembly if you intend to do something original.

PREPARE IN ADVANCE

In nearly all of these speeches for special occasions there will be names (of people and places), dates, and other essential details which must be included in your remarks. Check these thoroughly. It can be an embarrassment to all if you describe your guest incorrectly. It is imperative that you know how to pronounce the names properly—place-names need to be checked, as these can be a trap for the unwary.

CHECK PROTOCOL, TITLES, ETC.

On formal occasions you may have distinguished persons present which means that they should be introduced or welcomed in order of precedence.

Check with the civic centre to ensure that the person and his titles (or offices) are properly described, and stick to the form of address recommended by your authority.

BE BRIEF AND CONVINCING

A vote of thanks, an introduction, or a welcome usually requires only a short speech and, probably because of this, many speakers do not put much thought into what they say. Consequently, the same old clichés and worn-out phrases keep reappearing. The result is often a trite, dull, uninteresting monologue which (and this is its greatest flaw) conveys no genuine sentiment.

Whenever you have to make one of these speeches, make sure that what you say will be worth listening to, and let there be no doubt as to the sincerity of your purpose.

TOASTS AND SPEECHES AT WEDDINGS

Try to do more than just recall events in the lives of the bride and groom before you propose the toast. So often this reminiscing (entertaining as it may be to those who know the bride and bridegroom well, but meaningless to those on the fringe of the family group) becomes so long winded that it dominates the entire speech.

In such a toast you should try to say something of value, something in keeping with the occasion, something which, in later years, the young couple can look back on and clearly recall. It doesn't need to sound like a sermon; it doesn't need to be a doleful warning that life is not a bed of roses. What it needs is a touch of imagination and inspiration to lift it out of the dreary path of uniformity.

INTRODUCING A GUEST SPEAKER

Many speakers merely follow what others have done, without question or original thought. Take the following example:

'It is with pleasure that I introduce to members one who really needs no introduction at all.' (Notwithstanding this remark, he speaker then launches into a full-scale introduction.)

And what about this one:

'Our guest speaker today is Dr John Fox, who will shortly speak to us on The Crying Need for Water'. Dr Fox was born at Launceston, in 1921, and educated at the Melbourne Grammar School where he distinguished himself in the science laboratory and the football field, winning a scholarship which took him to Melbourne University. During the war years he served with the A.I.F. in North Africa and New Guinea, later taking up his studies again ...'

This type of introduction is all too common. It is a dull recital of academic, professional, or business achievements, and one can hardly be blamed for not listening with eager anticipation.

The requirements of a public introduction are virtually the same as for the everyday situation of bringing a stranger into a group of friends. The name is all-important and then a brief description of qualifications is necessary.

STRESS THE LINK BETWEEN SPEAKER AND AUDIENCE

The greatest need is to present some common ground for the group to be able to accept the newcomer quickly and easily. Example: 'May I introduce Ms Jeanne

Slavitt, Sales Director of X.Y.Z. Research Ltd , who is on her first visit to this country. She is particularly interested in underwater photography, and, incidentally, has quite a reputation as a writer of television plays.'

Whatever the circumstances, you still need to find something which makes it possible for speaker and audience to meet on common ground.

PERSONAL DETAILS

One problem that often arises is whether to give more attention to the speaker or their subject. The answer depends on the occasion. If the speaker is comparatively unknown, it is helpful to give more personal details. If the meeting is one which has had a continuing interest in the speaker's subject, little need be said about it. On the other hand, it could be helpful to indicate why this particular subject has been selected. A few words of warning:

1. Don't gild the lily

If the speaker is not 'one of our greatest authorities' and if their personal contribution does not 'rank with the greatest of any' then don't over-state the facts. It puts the speaker in an embarrassing position and sometimes he has to preface his speech with a few words of correction. No guest speaker should be forced to do this.

2. Don't talk about yourself

A recital of your own views or impressions of the speaker and his subject is not called for. You are speaking for the meeting, not for yourself. It's not you the audience has come to hear. It's the guest speaker.

3. Don't anticipate what the guest speaker may say

For example: 'I hope that Dr Fox will tell us, in his talk today, what the future holds for those in the far west.' This may be quite out of the context of the prepared address and, once again, the guest speaker may be disconcerted.

A VOTE OF THANKS

Speeches of this kind present one problem—you can't prepare much in advance, because you have no idea how successfully the guest speaker will carry out his task. But you will have time to make sure that you have names, titles, and so on quite correct and during the performance (whatever it may be) you should be alert for anything which will help you.

You can safely speak more personally in a vote of thanks, provided that what you say can be taken as the feeling of the audience. But don't do this: 'Listening to Dr Fox describing the damming of rivers I was reminded of . . .', followed by a personal anecdote. It might be fairly pertinent to the subject, but too many speakers make it into a supplementary speech, quite forgetting that they are supposed to be thanking the guest.

TACT
Perhaps the greatest problem facing any person who has to propose a vote of thanks arises when the performance was hardly adequate for the occasion. Great tact is needed.

HUMOUR
If the occasion is not strictly formal, some humour in your remarks will be appreciated. However, do not attempt to make fun of what the guest speaker has said.

SIMPLICITY

Remember that, as the proposer of a vote of thanks, your job is to thank the guest speaker adequately on behalf of the meeting. You can't go wrong if you express your appreciation simply and sincerely.

IMPROMPTU SPEECHES

There will be many times when you will want to say a few words without having had any chance to prepare your remarks beforehand, and it is not asking too much of any speaker to expect that his remarks should be worth listening to.

THINK CLEARLY

Most speakers have no trouble getting started, but a great many find it very difficult to develop their thoughts clearly and precisely. Very often they lose all sense of direction, which makes it almost impossible for them to bring their words to an effective conclusion. It is hard to think clearly because the mind must always be ahead of the voice.

BE AWARE OF THE EFFECT YOU ARE CREATING

When speaking impromptu, you can't give all your attention to thinking ahead (until you are an experienced and fluent speaker) because, if you do, you will have no control over your tongue. The result will be a speech peppered with 'ums' and 'ers'; seemingly never-ending sentences linked by the ubiquitous 'and', 'and also', and other conjunctions; and a dull and uninteresting delivery.

Discipline yourself to think clearly, to be able to form in your mind complete ideas, readily convertible into the spoken word, so that the listener does not have to suffer while you ramble on. Use short sentences at first and don't be afraid to have a small pause at each full stop. (If you don't, you'll start 'umming' and 'erring".)

Try to see the end of your speech long before you get to it. If you can do this, you will be able to choose the best way to develop your remarks so that they lead up to the conclusion.

PRACTISE

You can develop this skill by playing a little game. Ask someone to give you a subject and, after five seconds, you should say (1) how you would end your speech, (2) how you would begin it, (3) something of your remarks throughout.

If you play this game you will gradually develop the ability to plan the progress of your speech without a great deal of effort. The real test will come when you try to find the words to express your thoughts.

Use a tape-recorder so that you can listen carefully for grammatical errors and slovenly enunciation. Take particular note of the clarity (or otherwise) of your thoughts—do they convey to the listener a clear impression of what you had in mind? A speech without meaning or purpose, or one where the meaning is lost in a tangle of words or unconnected thoughts, gives the audience nothing. It's up to you, as the speaker, to give your listener something of value whenever you speak.

ONE LAST WORD

Public speaking groups are an opportunity to practice what you have studied. Do this and you'll be surprised how quickly you improve your ability to speak well in public.

PART 2: ADDRESSING PUBLIC MEETINGS, COMMITTEES AND THINK TANKS

INTRODUCTION

Men and women with outstanding achievements in professional, business, or academic fields often display limited ability when called upon to chair a or lead a discussion group.

This failure is often the result of ignorance of the qualifications required to be an effective chair of a meeting, or an acceptable leader of a discussion group. The skills needed for both roles are not the same. Good chairmen of meetings are often poor discussion leaders and vice versa.

A formal meeting led by an elected chair is governed by well-established procedures and rules of debate. A discussion group to be successful must be guided by its leader.

A good chair of a meeting restricts speakers to one, or at least a strictly limited number of, addresses; abd insists that all speeches are directed to, or through, the chair.

A discussion leader at a public meeting, on the other hand, encourages wide and free discussion among members in the group and tries to ensure that everyone present makes a contribution; and makes sure that his own participation is minimal.

Decisions are made at committee meetings through motions and voting and the chair may even give a casting vote when equal numbers support or reject a motion.

A discussion leader strives for acceptance of proposals by group agreement; and attempts to integrate the views of members into a statement that everyone will support.

The proceedings of a meeting are recorded in written minutes. The discussion leader makes progress summaries as the session advances and then develops a final summary with the help of all members of the group.

Well-run meetings and discussion groups help to achieve good community relationships. Unfortunately, on many occasions when people come together to talk for specific purposes, they fail because those who are selected to lead their deliberations do not understand their roles.

CHAIRING A MEETING

ELECTING A CHAIR

'First among equals' is a common definition for the chair of a meeting. At many meetings they take the chair automatically because of the position they occupy within the organisation—for example, as president of a club, or mayor of a district council, the managing director of the company. Rarely is their role challenged on these occasions.

There are, however, meetings where the first business is to elect a chair. When the matters to be discussed are likely to be controversial, those responsible for convening the meeting should ensure that the election of the chair is properly carried out.

When the meeting is ready to start, anyone may propose that a certain person present should be the interim or temporary chair for the purpose of electing a permanent chair for the meeting. Usually this suggestion is accepted without objection as the interim chair's role is a very short one.

The temporary chair should call for nominations for the permanent post for the meeting. The nomination should be made as a motion that 'Mr or Mrs X should be chair.' A seconder is required for the motion to be accepted; if there is no seconder, the motion lapses and another nomination is requested by the interim chair.

If only one name is proposed and seconded, the interim chair then puts the motion to the meeting and calls for a show of hands in favour and against. The motion will be declared 'carried' or 'lost.' If carried, the elected chair immediately takes over the conduct of the meeting; if the motion is lost on the show of hands, the temporary chair must call for further nominations.

If more than one nomination is moved, the temporary chair can then ask for a show of hands for each of the persons proposed and declare elected the one given the most votes.

Another way is to ask each person present to record his or her choice on a slip of paper. The papers are collected and checked by two tellers selected by those voting. The result is given to the temporary chair who announces the name of the person with most support.

If two or more nominations receive equal highest votes, it is better to suggest that the decision be made by some acceptable method—for example, by drawing a marked slip from a box or hat—than to ask the interim chair to give a casting or selective vote. They may be suspected of prejudice of some kind, particularly if it is known that they favour one of the candidates.

Although it is rarely done, it is possible for anyone at the meeting to propose or second himself for the chairship. If they do this, they can then vote for himself.

When the result of the election has been declared, the role of the temporary chair ceases and the chair is taken over by the successful candidate.

DUTIES AND RESPONSIBILITIES

A good chair recognises the importance of their role and ensures that, in addition to knowing their powers, they are well aware of their responsibilities. They must gain the respect of all present by carrying out his duties firmly, impartially, and in accordance with the rules of the particular body he or she is chairing or, if these guidelines do not exist, in conformity with accepted rules of meeting procedure.

Keeping order is undoubtedly a chair or president's major duty. Through lack of firmness, or ignorance of a rule of procedure, or inconsistent decisions, they can lose control of the meeting.

The first action is to ensure that there are enough people present to form a quorum if this is required. If the number is too few you should not allow the meeting to continue.

When minutes of a previous meeting have been prepared, the chair should ask for these to be read (or 'taken as read' if they have been circulated to all present). You should propose to the meeting that the minutes be confirmed and, if they are approved, you should sign and date them.

Whenever possible you should try to follow the order of the agenda for the meeting. You can, however, rearrange the order of items to be discussed.

As chair, you must ensure that all motions and amendments put forward are expressed in clearly understood terms and are related to the business before the meeting. Similarly, you must watch that all speakers keep to the point and confine their remarks to the content of the particular motion or amendment. If you feels confident of control, you may allow some flexibility in discussion.

Call upon speakers by name, taking care that on contentious matters you allow as many shades of opinion as possible to be expressed. You should not hesitate to insist that a speaker resume his seat if you believe that the speech is not dealing with the motion or amendment, or does not justify further time.

You should not permit speakers to be interrupted or allow private discussion among members. In keeping order the chair may find it necessary to warn a person who refuses to obey his ruling that, if you continues to offend, they may be asked to leave the meeting.

Make clear the method of voting to be used, give his own casting vote when there is an equal division of opinion, announce the results of a vote, decide on points of order, and close the meeting when you consider the time is appropriate.

Unless there is a contrary condition established in the rules governing the meeting, the chair may be removed at any time. Should someone propose a vote of no-confidence, the chair should warn those present that, if such a vote is carried, the meeting will be automatically adjourned. Instead, a motion should be proposed that a named person, other than the chair, take the chair. If the motion is carried, the newly elected chair takes the place of the former chair and the business continues.

THE QUOROM

Duly constituted meetings that are controlled by rules of procedure invariably specify that a minimum number of persons must be present before business can be dealt with. This minimum number is known as the quorum. At a small committee meeting the quorum may be as low as three; in other cases the rules may specify that at least one-third of the members of the full committee must be in attendance to constitute the quorum.

At some meetings more than the required quorum may be present, but ineligible persons cannot be counted as part of it. Unfinancial members, or other persons who may be present only because of their interest in the proceedings, but who are not entitled to vote, must be excluded by the chair when, at the start of the meeting, they checks whether or not there is sufficient attendance for a quorum.

Not only at the beginning of the meeting, but at any stage in its progress, the chair should be alert to the existence of a quorum. If there is not a quorum present, the meeting lapses, unless the rules governing the particular meeting specify otherwise.

The importance of the quorum is that, where the specific rules for the meeting require the attendance of a minimum number of persons, the meeting is not lawfully constituted and any business transacted is invalid if there are fewer than this number present.

It is not necessary that everyone present and qualified to vote should do so, unless the rules of the meeting require that a special majority for example, two-thirds of those in attendance—has to be achieved for a motion or amendment to be passed.

At meetings called for specific purposes and which are not connected with clubs or bodies governed by rules and regulations, the requirement of the quorum does not operate. The chair starts the meeting at the appointed time and completes the business of the agenda. Of course, if the number present is very small, with consequent little discussion, you may decide to end the meeting or adjourn it to another time.

PREPARING AN AGENDA
The dictionary definition of 'agenda' is 'things to be done'—and literally this is so. The agenda sets out the order of business to be covered at the meeting. Preparation of the agenda should not be a last-minute activity. The person responsible for its production should ensure that it contains sufficient information to indicate clearly the matters that the meeting proposes to discuss. The sequence of items is usually as follows:

1. Confirmation of minutes of the previous meeting.
2. Business arising from the minutes.
3. Consideration of reports and/or
4. Correspondence and new business.

An agenda may have as a final item 'Any other business,' but this is unnecessary, as any additional items can be introduced with the consent of the chair (if the rules governing the meeting permit this).

The success of a meeting can be affected by the information given on the agenda. If the names of those entitled to attend the meeting are known, it is as good practice to send them a copy of the agenda in advance, indicating clearly what has been planned for discussion. This information enables all who propose to attend to give some thought to the business of the meeting. The value of the discussion, and the decisions made, often reflect this pre-meeting consideration.

Many associations holding regular meetings stipulate that items for the agenda must be forwarded to the secretary a minimum number of days before the meeting. This proviso not only ensures that all persons attending know in advance what will be discussed but it also prevents the inclusion on the agenda of last-minute items. These late agenda entries may be both important and controversial. They may be suggested for discussion by their supporters when it is realised that there are not enough opponents of the proposals at the meeting to voice conflicting opinions or register contrary votes. An informative agenda circulated well before the meeting prevents these opportunistic tactics.

MOTIONS AND AMENDMENTS

You can easily lose control of the meeting, even with the understanding and support of most people present. This situation can usually be avoided if the chair is aware of some of the following requirements concerning motions and amendments:

1. The motion should be worded in clearly understood terms. To ensure this, the chair should insist, whenever possible, that the motion be presented to him in writing.
2. The motion should be expressed in positive and affirmative terms.
3. The chair should call on the mover of the motion to explain its object and what

they hope will be achieved if it is carried.

4. After the mover's explanation, the chair should ask for a seconder for the motion. The seconder may say, 'I second the motion, Mr Chair' and make no further comment, or you may speak in support of the motion.

5. The motion having been moved and seconded, the chair presents it to the meeting in the exact words of the mover and asks if anyone wishes to speak to the motion, for example:

'It has been moved and seconded 'that a donation of $100 be made to the XYZ Association to help in their building programme'.'

6. Those who wish to speak in support of, or against, the motion should then be permitted to do so. When several people rise at the same time the chair should quickly indicate who is to speak.

7. Any speaker who attempts to introduce into his speech material that is not relevant to the motion should be stopped immediately by the chair. He should be informed that his comments are out of order and that he must 'speak to the motion' if he wishes to continue.

8. When the discussion has ended or a time limit, if any, has expired, or there are no amendments, the chair should put the motion to the vote.

The chair will often be faced with amendments to the motion, particularly if a controversial subject is being discussed. The purpose of an amendment is to improve the motion. It should be framed so that it adds a word or words to the motion, or omits a word or words from the motion, or substitutes a word or words existing in the motion.

To avoid any misunderstanding, the chair should insist, whenever possible, that any amendment should be submitted in writing. You should not accept any amendment until the motion has been moved and seconded and you should refuse an amendment that is a direct negative of the motion or one that introduces an entirely different proposal. Those who completely reject the motion have the opportunity of expressing their opposition when the motion is put to the vote.

In a heated debate a number of amendments may be proposed. Under pressure a chair may decide to accept more than one amendment at the same time, but you run the risk of confusing members and possibly losing control of the meeting. There is, however, no reason why a member should not indicate that you intends later to propose an amendment different from the one being discussed. Such information is often helpful to the chair and other members.

FORMAL MOTIONS

In the course of a meeting the chair may be confronted by what is termed a 'formal motion.' Formal motions may be proposed without any prior notice from the mover. The mover of a formal motion has no right of reply. Formal motions may be proposed to stop the discussion and force a vote, to prevent a vote from being taken, to postpone further discussion until the next meeting or a definite time and place. The chair needs to be prepared for these motions, and adjust the meeting accordingly.

Taking the vote

The voting procedure for meetings is often set out in the rules of various organisations. Where this is so the chair must, of course, abide by the direction. At many meetings, however, the chair will have the power to take the vote as you thinks fit. The most common methods you may use are below.

Voices

At the appropriate time the chair may say, 'I propose to put the motion [or amendment]. All those in favour say `Aye'; to the contrary 'No'. Assesses the volume of verbal support, both for and against, and declare the proposal carried or lost.

The chair should have no doubts about the decision when voting is by voices. Often a minority will make more sound than the opposing majority and the chair may be misled. It is also possible that the chair may be challenged on the correctness of his interpretation of the vocal vote. In all such cases, you should not hesitate to call immediately for a show of hands to decide the issue.

Show of hands

With this method the chair asks all in favour of the motion to raise the right hand. Counts the hands and then ask those who are against the motion to indicate their wish in the same way. If the division of opinion is quite obvious, will indicate the result of the vote, sometimes stating the numbers for and against the being voted on. If the vote is a close one, the chair may call for two tellers to assist him in the count. The tellers should be representative of affirmative and negative sides and should agree with each other, and the chair, on the result of the count.

Ballot

Because of the number present at the meeting, or a requirement of the organisation concerned, or a desire to keep individual voting secret, a vote on a motion or on another matter, may be decided by ballot. Those present at the meeting indicate their views on slips of paper by writing 'yes' or 'no.' When a secret vote is being taken, it is wise to print on the voting paper, or write on a screen for all to read, the exact words of the proposal to be decided on. Scrutineers from each side check the votes, agree on the totals, and pass the figures to the chair, who announces the result to the meeting. Usually, the chair will reveal the actual strength for and against the motion, but some chairmen will merely indicate that the motion has been won or lost.

Casting vote

The chair has the right to both an ordinary—sometimes called 'original' —vote and a casting vote. If they decides to use their ordinary vote, they should do so when the fellow members are voting on the motion; you should not wait until you can see how the wind is blowing before exercising that right.

Many chairs are not happy about giving a casting vote. Often they will suggest to the meeting that the proposal should be discussed further and a second vote taken, in the hope that a tie will not then result. If voting is again equal, the chair can still decline to indicate his view. If you do make a casting vote, you may vote as you wish, but most good chairs believe that a casting vote should maintain the existing situation, rather than bring about a change.

ADJOURNMENTS

The decision to adjourn a meeting to another date usually comes from the members present. If a majority is in favour of this action, the chair should conform with their wishes through a resolution from the meeting. Many organisations, however, have rules that empower a chair to adjourn a meeting for a short time and leave the chair, if control is becoming difficult, because of unruly behaviour or heated discussion. When tempers have cooled, you can then call the meeting to order and continue the business.

Should a chair leave the chair against the wish of the majority present, or without powers that enable him to do so, the meeting is not adjourned. Provided that a quorum, if this is required, is present, these persons can elect a new chair and continue the meeting.

An adjourned meeting is considered a continuation of the previous meeting. Invariably, only business unfinished from the earlier meeting is dealt with, and no new business is transacted.

The adjournment may be to a definite date or to a time to be fixed later. It may be adjourned to the same or another place. Notice should be given to all eligible members of the time, date, and place of the adjourned meeting, as was the case with the original meeting.

KEEPING MINUTES

A record of the proceedings of every meeting should be kept. This record—the minutes—is always written by the secretary of the organisation holding the meeting, or by some other person approved by the members present.

Minutes must be complete yet concise, accurate, expressing only facts (and not the writer's opinions), and set out in such a way that ready reference can be made at any time to any item discussed.

The minutes should indicate clearly the particular nature of the meeting—annual, weekly, special, general, and so on—and give the date, time, and place. The name of the chair should be given and, where the number is small (as at a committee meeting), the names of all present should be recorded. At large meetings, names (apart from that of the chair) are unnecessary in the minutes, but the number present should be shown.

The business of the meeting should be set down in chronological order, starting with the election of the chair—if this occurs—followed by the confirmation of minutes of the preceding meeting and then by a record of each item dealt with.

Precise wording should be used to list any decisions made. Motions and amendments should be stated clearly and an indication given as to whether they were carried or lost. The names of movers and seconders can be given, although this is frequently not done.

Numbers for and against a proposal need not be listed, unless the rules of the meeting state that certain motions must be carried by a prescribed majority of votes. When contentious matters have been discussed and it is considered that differing points of view should be minuted, it is essential that the recording should be strictly accurate and objective. In no sense must the minute writer express their own opinion. You should ensure that opposing statements by speakers are given relative space and importance.

There is no doubt that many minutes of meetings are 'loaded.' A dozen or more lines may be given in the minutes to the statements of 'Mr A' — whose views the minute writer supports—and one line, 'Mr B also spoke,' to the opposing speaker. While such a minute is not inaccurate, it is certainly unfair. A good chair watches for slanted recording of this kind and has a private talk with the secretary on improved recording; you must, however, exercise great care himself in giving such advice—a resentful minute writer may complain that the chair has subjected him to unfair pressure.

After the meeting, the secretary, in addition to writing the minutes, should take prompt action on any decisions that you was instructed to act upon the writing of letters, payment of money, personal contacts with institutions or individuals.

COMMITTEES

A cynic once said that committees were made up of the unfit and appointed by the incompetent to do the unnecessary. Despite this hard criticism which may be true occasionally, there is little doubt that the use of committees has increased in all forms of organisations.

Committees should justify their existence in quality of decisions made as well as in terms of time and money. They are without exception appointed for specific tasks. Provided that appropriate persons are selected for membership and the objectives of operation are clearly defined, committees can be worthwhile.

Only matters likely to be better handled by group discussion rather than by individual action warrant delegation to a committee Where positive leadership is required, this is the role for an individual; where wide and differing views of qualified people need co-ordinating, committees may be best.

Any organisation or meeting deciding to set up a committee should be guided by some basic rules.

BASIC RULES FOR COMMITTEES

1. Determine the proper size of the committee. With more than twelve members the committee becomes a crowd; with less than four, the value of group discussion can be limited.
2. Be specific as to the task to be carried out by the committee. Preferably, the terms of reference should be defined in writing. Rarely should a general brief be given.
3. Appoint only members who, because of their qualifications, background, and interest, are likely to make a worthwhile contribution to the committee's work.
4. Keep the level of membership as uniform as possible. Frank discussion and provocative views are not likely in a company committee where the general manager

and a junior clerk are members, or in a sporting club committee where a senior coach and a new recruit find themselves on opposite sides of the table. Freedom of expression is essential in getting results.

5. Decide whether the committee is to be given an executive or advisory role. If it has powers to implement its decisions, care should be taken to ensure that such action warrants group authority. It is most unwise to force a committee to carry out a decision that is obviously the responsibility of an individual. Most committees perform an advisory function.

6. When possible, set a timetable for results; otherwise committee discussions can continue far beyond the time they justify. Pressure to meet a deadline can develop concentrated and economical thinking.

7. When the committee makes its recommendations, try and act on them. If the right members have been appointed, they should be qualified to give the best advice. Speedy implementation of its report is the best reward for any committee. Vacillation over accepting its ideas by people not so well qualified as the committee members will soon dampen their enthusiasm.

ELECTION OF OFFICERS

Most organised bodies elect their officers once a year, generally at their annual general meeting. Ample time should be given for the calling of nominations and for consideration by members of the qualifications of those who have been proposed for office.

In some cases voting takes place at the annual meeting by a show of hands. When the number of nominations exceeds the vacant offices to be filled, a ballot is held.

Another method aimed at ensuring that all eligible members have the opportunity to vote, whether or not they attend the annual meeting, is to send each member a voting slip. On the top half of the slip the names of all nominations are set out in alphabetical order; on the bottom half is a line for the voter's signature.

At the appropriate time, often just before, or in the early period of, the annual meeting, the plain envelopes are opened by scrutineers. They count the votes and pass the results to the chair who announces the names of the successful candidates. Sometimes you will give the actual voting figures, but many chairmen will omit this information if they feel the limited support given to some candidates may cause embarrassment if made public.

LEADING A DISCUSSION OR THINK TANK

A group discussion or think tank is a meeting of people who pool their experiences and ideas. The aim is usually to solve a problem or mutually to agree on a conclusion on the topic before them.

A discussion group should consist of not more than ten to fifteen persons and all should have had some background or experience that qualifies them to make positive and constructive contributions on the propositions to be discussed.

No motions are put forward or votes taken in a group discussion. From the often surprising wealth of knowledge that soon becomes obvious when a group of people with related interests meet together, a final statement is evolved that includes the best thinking of all present.

It is unnecessary to have complete agreement in a group discussion; indeed, many successful conferences of this kind can end in a statement of sincerely held differences of opinion. In such situations, these informational discussions can provide far more valuable data for those who have to make final decisions than if they were given merely the result of a majority motion.

The experience of taking part in a well-prepared group discussion, under a competent leader, can stimulate a participant's thinking, add to his knowledge, and develop him for more important roles in life. You will be called upon to analyse the views of other people, to try to understand the reasons for their opinions, and then to question the validity of your own conclusions.

In discussions of various subjects the leader becomes aware of facts that were unknown, discovers advantages and disadvantages in both his own and in other people's attitudes, and appreciates the value of well-reasoned decisions, as opposed to snap, emotional 'hunches.'

The established rules of debate with motions, amendments, and other procedures do not apply in group discussion. The problem or matter for discussion is clearly stated by the leader at the start of the session and then follows a free exchange of ideas by all present. The leader, of course, maintains orderly control of the discussion, but you should encourage the expression of the widest range of opinions relevant to the topic before the session.

Provided that only one person speaks at a time, all persons present may address others at the meeting without going through the leader. They may ask questions, they may agree or disagree with other opinions, and they may suggest solutions to problems without the leader coming into the discussion unless you feels it is necessary to do so.

A group discussion in the form of a meeting or conference may be held for many reasons. An organisation at a general meeting may decide to set up a special committee to examine and make recommendations on some specific topic.

A manager or a departmental head may delegate to a group of selected staff members the task of solving a particular problem, or recommending a course of action, or examining the merits of a specific proposition.

Group discussions of this kind are often established by organisations in an attempt to achieve reconciliation between sections holding strong differences of opinion.

Another form of discussion group may be set up for information gathering purposes. The aim may be to give a better understanding to all those involved in the introduction of a new method or technique, or a proposed change in existing procedures. When decimal currency was introduced in several countries, many business and public organisations set up discussion groups of employees with the aim of conveying an appreciation of all aspects of the financial change.

In fact, any group wanting to know more about a subject, or to solve a problem, or achieve agreement on a disputed matter among people of related interests, may well decide that a group discussion is their best course of action.

DISCUSSION LEADER

The key person in the success of any group session is the leader. Only a competent leader will get worthwhile results from the group; indeed if you lack the skills of discussion leadership you can easily create confusion and discord among those at the meeting.

Often it is unwise to allow the group to select its own leader. You may be the most popular among them, you may have a reputation for being a good chair of meetings, you may be the most senior in status in the group, but you may still be an ineffective discussion leader.

Those responsible for setting up the group meeting should consider carefully the qualifications of the leader. They should acquaint themselves with the basic requirements of the role and then choose the best person available.

The discussion method of leadership does not call for an expert in the subject to be dealt with. Certainly the more knowledge you has of the subject to be discussed the better, but many successful leaders are less informed on the topic than most members in their group.

The following are certain positive qualities that a good leader should possess:

Open-mindedness

You must create a climate in the group where there is complete confidence in your fairness and lack of prejudice on any point discussed. In fact it is essential that you do not indicate which way your sympathies lie even when challenged. You should not attempt in any way to influence the group to think in a certain direction. You must not pose as an authority on any point raised, although you may suggest that consideration be given to pertinent aspects of the matter being discussed if you believes such attention to be worthwhile.

Clear, quick thinking

Particularly when the discussion is moving at a rapid rate, the leader must be one step ahead. You must assess quickly the direction of the discussion, noting signposts in the comments of members that indicate whether progress is being made towards a solution, or the introduction of side issues that may cloud the main business. You must anticipate likely difficulties before they occur and take measures to avoid their development. For example, you may believe that the increasing difference of views between several sections in the group is becoming so marked that, unless the discussion is switched along different lines, statements may be made that could create an impasse in the meeting. In such a situation you might tactfully interrupt the discussion and suggest that members try another line of thinking.

Alternatively, if it appears that the discussion is making no progress through lack of understanding, or insufficient knowledge on the matter before the group, the leader may inject a comment, or suggest consideration of some factual data that you have available.

Fluent speech

The group leader must know how to express himself succinctly, using the right words at the right time. In presenting the problem for discussion you must do so in terms that are clearly understood by all present. As the meeting proceeds you should make brief summaries at appropriate intervals. By doing so, you assist the thinking of members of the group and make them realise how they are progressing.

Some members of discussion groups have difficulty in expressing themselves. When necessary, the leader, without making it obvious that you are doing so, should recast statements made by members, or questions asked, in terms more clearly understood. A speaker may make a long, ambiguous statement, which may puzzle others present or create misunderstanding. The leader, in this situation, might say, 'You obviously feel, Mr 'X', that what should be done is this . . .' (here the leader rephrases the speaker's awkwardly expressed comments in brief, lucid terms).

Skill at analysis

If you have prepared yourself before the group meeting by a study of material concerning the topic to be discussed, you will almost certainly know what you hopes to accomplish. Throughout the discussion you must then ensure, without making this aim too obvious, that all present work towards this final objective. This can be done, even with wide disagreement on some aspects of the subject under discussion, provided that the leader analyses each contribution and selects those parts that will help in reaching a worthwhile conclusion. This skill can be likened to that required of a factory worker whose job it is to take from a moving conveyor belt, holding a miscellaneous collection of items, the essential parts of a certain product.

Personal qualities

As with all those who are called on to lead others, there is an unlimited number of personal qualities that a good discussion leader should possess to ensure success, but such paragons of virtue are rare. There are, however, several characteristics that you should cultivate.

Be tactful and diplomatic in dealing with the members of the group, making sure that no-one is hurt or embarrassed by your comments. Be patient with the slow-thinking, firm but courteous with the arrogant and 'know-alls,' encourage the shy or nervous and show courage when forced to take a line of action to maintain control over the meeting.

Experience in group and conference leading will soon give you confidence that will earn the respect of those whom you is called upon to guide. The qualities listed cannot be injected into a man or woman like a dose of penicillin, but they can be developed by those who realise what is required and who set about improving their skill by practice.

PREPARING THE DISCUSSION

The leader's preparation must not be a last-minute effort. It calls for timely consideration and detailed planning of all the factors that make for successful group discussions.

First, the leader must define the terms of the topic or problem to be discussed. and determine the exact objective of the meeting —for example, to find a solution to a particular difficulty, to attempt a reconciliation of varying points of view, to disseminate information to interested members.

With this objective clearly understood, you should then do some research on the topic to be discussed and assemble as much relevant information as possible. It could be that others present at the meeting will be better informed than the leader on various matters raised in the discussion, but this superior knowledge need pose no problem for the leader, if it is obvious to the group members that you have done some worthwhile 'homework' in gather pertinent data.

From the facts assembled the leader should prepare a meeting or discussion guide. This is a written plan in which you sets down his outline for leading the discussion. In formulating this guide knowledge about those who will attend the session is important. If you are aware of their individual strengths and weaknesses, and their likely attitudes, you can prepare for handling possible developments— especially difficult ones.

In analysing the discussion topic, the leader should determine the relative importance of points that you consider should be covered. Include a provisional timetable in which you allot approximate periods for dealing with the various points. Without this schedule you may find that too much time is being given to less important matters in the early stage of the discussion and that more vital issues have to be rushed through in the final minutes of the meeting.

A brief introductory statement must be prepared. It should welcome the members, state clearly the objective of the session, ask for their co-operation and constructive participation and, if necessary, explain concisely some of the important requirements for successful group discussion. This introduction may end with a question, to start the members talking.

The group leader should anticipate how the discussion is likely to proceed. The plan should consider possible group reactions if certain problems do arise and you should decide how you will handle such issues.

These situations may call for firm control during periods of heated discussion, or the need to arouse interest when members are showing a lack of enthusiasm in the proceedings. In both cases you can reveal leadership skill by asking appropriately prepared questions, suggesting another line for discussion, or by making a brief summary of what has been achieved to that stage.

Use visual aids to stimulate the discussion, for example charts, statistical data or projections.

Try to ensure, whether or not it is your responsibility, that all physical requirements for the session are satisfactory. This means that the meeting place is suitable—well-lit, appropriately ventilated, with acceptable seating—and that written materials and facilities for using visual aids are available. Seeing that these are in order can make the difference between the success or otherwise of the meeting.

LEADING THE MEETING

The meeting should start on time. Prepared name-cards are used at many meetings.

These are pieces of white card or stiff paper about A4 in size, scored lengthwise down the middle, and bent into the shape of a tent. The name of each member is printed on both sides of the card, in large letters for all to read.

The leader should confirm the reason for the meeting. You should state the topic to be discussed and the objectives it is hoped to achieve. Below is a sample discussion guide prepared by a leader required to lead a two-hour session with the aim of improving the standard of communication within a company.

DISCUSSION MEETING GUIDE

Topic: Communication in the Company

Objectives:
1. Keeping staff better informed.
2. Encouraging upward communication.
3. Overcoming communication barriers.

Timetable:

2.00 p.m. Introductory comments.

2.05 Analysis of present situation.

2.20 Show film, The Grapevine.

2.40 Suggestions for improving communication.

3.20 Recommendation Plan for management.

3.50 Final summary

Equipment:

Projector and screen. Film: The Grapevine.

Organisation charts.

Note pads, pencils, clock.

Questions:

Who is responsible for what information?

Who should be informed of what ?

How can lines of upward communication be improved?

What forms of communication should be used?

What barriers exist in present upward and downward communication processes in the Company?

The leader should ask for the co-operation of all participants in achieving the aim of the meeting. Emphasize that the session is one of discussion, in which the views of everyone will be sought. Not only should all present express their own opinion freely, but they should listen courteously and attentively to the contributions of fellow members.

The leader should explain briefly his role to introduce the discussion, to ensure that it is making progress towards its objectives, and to encourage every member to take an active part in the proceedings. You may indicate that from time to time you will introduce relevant facts, if considered helpful, and you may ask questions to stimulate discussion.

Members should be told that the leader is not 'there as an expert or an authority on the topic to be discussed'. You should emphasize that you will not take a partisan role in the discussion, or indicate in any way your own opinions—even if asked by members to do so. You will summarize discussion as the meeting progresses and at the end you will make a final summary with the assistance of all members. There will be no voting and all decisions reached must be an agreed opinion of the group.

To start the discussion, the leader will often ask a question of the group. For example, the meeting may have been called to discuss ways of improving communications within an organisation. After introductory remarks, the leader may say 'I suggest that we start by asking 'Who is responsible in our company for issuing information to new staff joining us?' The leader could be more provocative by asking, 'Is there anything wrong with the communication process in our company and, if so, what?'

Once the members are talking freely and keeping to the subject, the leader should say as little as possible. You can allow members to address each other without going through him as leader. Although the leader's comments should be few you must, of course, listen intently to the development of the discussion and take action immediately if the situation demands it. The following are situations that warrant the leader's intervention:

When discussion moves away from the main topic

In this case the leader can say, 'What we are discussing is of interest, but it might be better if, in order to achieve our objectives, we asked ourselves this question, [and then give an example].' Bring the discussion back into line by posing a question that is relevant to the main topic.

When there is uneven discussion

Most meetings have members who have a lot to say and others who are reluctant to express their opinions. Unless the leader is alert and firm, the meeting can quickly develop into a monopoly of discussion by several members. When this happens, the leader should interject in a quiet, non-critical manner and say, 'We have heard the views of several who obviously feel strongly about the subject we are discussing; I suggest that we here from those who have not yet spoken, as their experience and opinions could be of value to us.'

A response chart is often used by discussion leaders. This is a sheet of paper with the names of all the members taking part in the discussion written on it. As each one speaks, the leader places a mark, such as a tick or a cross, opposite his name. In this way you can see clearly those members who are doing most of the talking and those who are silent. By tactfully restraining the loquacious participants, and encouraging the less vocal ones, a better balance of discussion can be achieved.

When the statements made are obviously wrong

Sometimes, because of ignorance, or intentionally, a member may introduce into the discussion material that the leader knows is misleading or incorrect. When this happens the leader, at a break in the member's flow of words, may interrupt by saying, 'We must be sure that the statements you are making are correct because they do affect our discussion. Can you give us facts to support what you say?'

Alternatively, the leader may have prepared material that contradicts the incorrect assertions. When this is so, intervention can be, 'I thought this point might come up and I have some facts here that might help us.'

Misleading or incorrect statements often bring challenges from other members of the group. The leader should handle these interruptions carefully. You should not allow a heated discussion to ensue, but suggest that it seems as if some members have information that may not be known to the person making the misleading comments. This suggestion can save embarrassment for the member who has been challenged, as you can grasp the opportunity to claim that you were unaware of the facts produced by those who corrected him.

When discussion is too fast

This does not happen very often but it can occur when some members are better informed on the discussion topic than others. An attentive leader will sense that the discussion is moving too quickly for some of the group, that they are failing to grasp the full weight of statements being made and may be reticent to reveal this lack of understanding. The leader should not hesitate in such situations to interrupt the discussion and ask for clearer comments, or more detailed facts, so that all members can fully appreciate what is being said.

Another way to slow down discussion is to suggest that the time is appropriate to make a summary of progress to date. The leader may well ask the speaker to frame the words of this summary.

When discussion can be embarrassing

Embarrassing situations can quickly arise. A member may break a confidence and reveal facts that the leader believes should not be made public. Pointed or indirect criticism may be made of persons outside the group. Members may refer in derogatory terms to matters of nationality, religion, politics, or personal beliefs and be unaware that they are causing offence to other people in the group.

Whether such statements are intentional or not, the leader should not allow them to continue. You should interrupt the speaker and point out that their comments must cease as they may be regarded as a breach of confidence, or be unfair, or embarrassing to persons present or not present.

The leader must be particularly careful to maintain a strictly neutral attitude in such situations and not indicate in any way his own feelings on the statements made. Privately you may agree with the embarrassing comment, but no one in the group should be aware of this.

SUMMING UP DURING THE MEETING

As the meeting continues, the leader should summarise the discussion at appropriate stages. You can do this when proceedings are not moving quickly enough, when you wish to slow down the discussion or when the members do not seem to be grasping the real aim of the session. However, the time for a brief summary is usually at that point when the leader considers that members should review the ground they have covered and agree on their progress.

Short summaries made by the leader at appropriate breaks throughout the discussion can help in getting the co-operation and consent of all members when the final summation is made. It is in this effort that the leader shows his skill. The summary should be positive and constructive. It may be necessary to make some critical comment in it, but little is achieved by a recital of negative views; wherever possible there should be recommendations or suggestions made for practical actions as a result of what has come out of the discussion.

The final summary should be written on a screen or sheet of paper for all members to read and agree to. It is possible to have a valuable discussion that can end in a disagreement of views among members. Provided that the summary indicates fairly and objectively this lack of unanimity, the meeting can still be considered to have been worthwhile.

Using questions to move the discussion forward

The value of the right kind of question at the right time cannot be over-estimated in achieving success in the session. Good leaders prepare their questions with careful thought as to their use and they direct them in a form that will bring the most effective response. Questions may be asked by the leader for a number of reasons.

1. To start discussion

This can be the leader's first move to get the discussion going, after you has made his introductory remarks. The question should be well- thought-out and aimed at getting a positive, early response from the group. A weak question, with no stimulating content, can have a marked dampening effect on the opening of the discussion.

2. To end, or change direction of, discussion

The leader may consider that sufficient time has been given to a certain aspect of the discussion. Rather than tell the group that you has come to this decision, and that they should end or change the direction of their thinking, you can interrupt with an appropriate question, such as, 'We have had some good discussion on this angle of our subject, but what are your views on . . . ?' (here you introduce a new point for discussion). With skilful wording, a leader can use this question without upsetting the group. In many cases members do not sense the reason for his interruption and they take up the discussion on the new approach as you suggests.

3. To gain information

The leader may consider that some of the group have information which could help the discussion but which has not been made known. You may also believe that a particular member, because of his background or experience, could assist the meeting if they were encouraged to develop their ideas. In these situations, the leader either asks the members as a group for the details you seeks, or invites the specific member to supply the information.

4. To improve the level of discussion

Group meetings and conferences can be expensive sessions when the time and salary costs of those taking part are counted. Decisions made should be worthy of the calibre of the persons involved. However, it often happens that unless the leader is alert, the discussion can deteriorate to a level well below what should be expected from those taking part.

This falling away in quality may be caused by the speakers' lack of interest, or obsession with aspects of the subject warranting only minor attention but given far too much time, or by clashes of personalities that lower the value of individual contributions. A good leader senses the development of a low-level discussion. They quickly inject questions to provoke a higher standard of thinking and stimulate exchanges more worthy of the composition of the particular group. Preparation of questions of suitable quality is an essential pre-requisite for successful group meetings.

5. To widen participation

Inexperienced or shy members may be reluctant to hear the sound of their own voices. When the leader notices this silence you can ask a question to bring the member into the discussion, but it must be a question that the modest member can answer well.

TYPES OF QUESTIONS

The value of the question in a group discussion is that it calls for an answer. However, the same form of question should not be used for all situations. A skilful leader selects one of four recognised types of questions to get the best response:

1. The overhead question

The leader directs this question to the members as a group. Anyone may answer it, but, if the leader feels that the reply is not a good one, you may look around the room for further responses. The overhead question is the one most often used to start discussion, unless the leader considers more value would be gained by asking someone in particular to speak first.

2. The direct question

As implied, this type of question is asked of a particular member. The leader may use it when you wishes the member to speak because of his knowledge of the subject, or to bring into the discussion someone whose attention appears to be wandering. The direct question is also appropriate to encourage a nervous or difficult person who may appear reluctant to speak. The direct question should be used by the leader with care and forethought. If wrongly used, it can cause embarrassment and resentment because of the member's inability to answer it, or because they do not expect to be asked it. Invariably a good leader will first call the name of the member to whom you propose to ask the direct question, thus giving him time to collect his thoughts as the question is being put to him. There are occasions, however, when because of lack of interest by members in the discussion, the leader will ask the direct question, naming the person to answer it as the final word. This tactic certainly secures the attention of the group as they all wait to here whether or not they are the selected respondent!

3. The reverse question

During discussion on disputed issues a member may ask the leader for his opinion. The leader must realise that, they may quickly become involved in the discussion as an obvious partisan. You should quickly reverse the question to the asker by saying, 'What do you think?' or, if you believe the questioner has not the knowledge to give a satisfactory answer, you can use the relay question.

4. The relay question

In this situation you repeat, or reframe, the question in more suitable words and gives it to the group in overhead or direct form. It is important that the leader should ask his questions in concise and clear language. There must be no misunderstanding of his purpose. In so doing you will encourage informative and unambiguous answers. The question should challenge the thinking of the member, but not be so difficult that you find it too hard to answer.

PROBLEMS FOR THE DISCUSSION LEADER

Even the best planned discussion meeting can run into trouble through unexpected situations developing from group reactions, or from difficulties with individual members. A good leader is not upset by these events; you can show your calibre by the calm and competent way you handle these occurrences.

Lack of interest
A lethargic group may have a number of causes—conviction that the topic being discussed is of little importance, a feeling that whatever is decided upon will not be implemented, or the knowledge or suspicion that a decision by higher authority has already been made and the meeting is merely a ruse to claim that advice has been sought from the group. It is also possible that a dislike of the group leader, or the presence of some senior colleague who would resent views contrary to his own, will inhibit discussion.

These are formidable obstacles to successful group leading but, in most situations, they can be overcome by a leader with the necessary moral courage. If the topic does not appear to interest the group, the leader should introduce a related theme that you knows will encourage a more active response. Often this move will start debate and at an appropriate time the leader can, through well directed questions, bring the discussion back to the planned topic.

While the group may suspect that their recommendations are not likely to be put into practice, an enthusiastic leader can often convince them that really worthwhile proposals might well gain acceptance. The group should not accept defeat without first fighting the battle to get its ideas implemented.

Similarly, when members believe that a decision has already been made on the matter being discussed, and that their meeting is simply a formality to prove that the group advice has been sought, all is not lost. It is true, for example, that some determined managers find group consultations irksome. They will make up their own minds without help, but many decided actions have been amended, or even reversed, as the result of solid arguments from an interested group who feel strongly on the subject.

Dislike of a group leader, or reluctance to express opinions before a senior colleague, may show in an apparent lack of interest by members. A good leader often induces the group to start talking by asking a question that they know members can answer because of their specialized knowledge or interest, or a provocative one that they believe will stimulate ready response. You may even make an intentional false statement to bring a quick rebuttal; if this happens, you can then ask members to explain more fully where you is wrong.

Discussion out of control

This can happen in a matter of seconds and the leader must move quickly to regain command of the situation. The topic being discussed may be a highly controversial one or there may be strong personal dislikes between members. Heated arguments may ensue.

The group leader can often regain control by suggesting that the particular aspect being debated be left for the time being and that another line of discussion be considered. You can ask a general question or a direct one to a member to achieve this result. If there is a screen in the room, you may stand up and suggest that a summary of points discussed to that stage should be recorded; this action often cools tempers. If these moves fail you can calmly but firmly call for order, pointing out that no matter how strongly members feel about their views, progress will not be made unless there is reasoned and objective discussion. In the last resort, if the meeting continues to be unruly, you should decide on a short break. What is important is that, no matter how the situation develops, you should not relinquish leadership control.

Lack of interest by the group as a whole, or a display of heated argument around the table, is often sparked off by the actions of one member. Individual behaviour, while not bringing group reaction, can still challenge the leader's competence. Among difficult members may be some of the following:

The side-talker

This member sometimes converses with his neighbours in low tones on the subject being discussed, but often his comments have nothing to do with the meeting. In any case this action distracts the attention of the group. The leader should look directly at the offender and often this deliberate notice will be sufficient to stop the discourtesy. Should this indication not succeed, the leader should call the offender by name and ask him a relevant question, or seek his opinion on the views of a member who has previously spoken.

If 'side-talking' becomes too frequent, the leader should stop the group discussion. You should then state that the value of the meeting will be lost if members do not give all their attention to the person who is speaking and that in any case it is discourteous to the meeting to carry on private discussion. Members soon sense that the leader will not tolerate these distractions.

The over-talker

A group member who tries to dominate the discussion may do so because they feel very strongly about the subject, or because they are naturally a voluble person. They must, however, be restricted to a fair contribution and the leader should achieve this end without, if possible, embarrassing him.

You can interrupt the talkative member by thanking him for his comments but pointing out that you would like to hear the views of other members in order to get as wide a range of opinions as possible. The leader can also ask the offender a difficult question that may stop his flow of words. A good leader can become quite skilled in failing to notice a member who wishes to speak too often or too long.

Experience at many discussion groups shows that fellow members will take care of any of their number who try to monopolize the proceedings. They show by their irritation how much they resent unwarranted interruptions or lengthy statements. In extreme cases the leader may be compelled to have a private talk with the 'over-talker' outside the meeting room and politely ask him to limit his contributions.

The non-talker

Shy or inarticulate members can pose problems for the leader. They may be embarrassed when called upon to speak and yet they should contribute to justify their membership of the group. The leader can bring them into the discussion by asking questions that you are sure they can answer or you can invite them to comment on matters in which you know they have had experience. Through a tactful compliment on the view expressed, the leader can encourage the timid member to take a more active part in the discussion.

The grievance-airer

Some people welcome inclusion in a discussion group as an opportunity to air their personal complaints about matters that may or may not have any relevance to the topic being dealt with. Others may upset fellow members by using the discussion to criticise or to argue with them over imagined or real grievances.

When such situations develop, the leader must indicate that the meeting is not the place for such expressions. You can invite the member concerned to discuss his grievance with him privately after the meeting. You must insist that no personal criticisms of persons present or outside the meeting can be allowed. In large organisations, where staff discussion groups are set up, the leader must be watchful that criticism—implied or direct—of superiors does not become a focal point of the session. It is possible that criticism of the actions of persons outside the room may be made in the group discussion, but the leader must not allow this line to develop. Discussion groups are not trials by jury.

The arguer

Progress can be slowed down in a discussion if a member shows a determination to differ with his leader, or with fellow members, on points of minor importance. Often the group will deal with this type of person by showing their impatience with his attitude. However, the leader must not allow this criticism to become too personal. You should indicate that worthwhile results will not be achieved unless positive and helpful contributions are made by all present. If this approach is unsuccessful, you should speak to the member after the meeting and point out that his actions do not help the discussion.

Increasing competence in discussion leading can be achieved by critical self-analysis. Constructive help in evaluating one's performance can be invited from friends or members of the group, but comments offered are not always true!